little Saints of the Liberties

by
Malachy Cullen, O.S.A.

IRISH MESSENGER PUBLICATIONS
37 Lower Leeson Street,
Dublin 2.

Cover design and illustrations by Niamh Foran.

With ecclesiastical permission: Patrick O'Connell, S.J.
                                 Censor. Theol. Deput.
Dublin: 19th June 1991.

ISBN 1 872245 16 1
5-11-91

Printed in the Republic of Ireland by
Colour Books Limited, Dublin.

CONTENTS

Little Saints of the Liberties 5

Chosen Out 7

The Mother 10

I Can't Pray 11

The Quart of Water 12

My Shame 14

From the Ends of this Earth 14

Is It Any Harm? 16

Dolores 18

Monica 20

The Blackberry Pickers 22

Vision 24

Her Preparations Made 25

On Being a Priest 28

Reunion 30

LITTLE SAINTS OF THE LIBERTIES

*N*owadays everybody is talking about the Liberties of Dublin. Quaint little houses are being converted into trendy town houses; swanky, new apartments are going up all over the place. Old but fashionable; full of antiques: it's the 'in' place to live.

It's a pity how little these new residents know of the old Liberties. The old Liberties were *people*: people who were always poor; often hungry, often holy, but always loving and lovable. In fact, they were the most loving and lovable people on earth.

I had the good fortune to live with these people for the first six months of 1942. I was based in the Augustinian Priory in John's Lane and I was waiting for a ship to take me to Africa, for the War was going on there. And I can tell you, when my ship was ready to leave I left the Liberties with bleeding roots. My heart was sunk there.

Home after ten years, I was once again posted to John's Lane to write the mission magazine. (I had been good at compositions in school!) That was in 1952. Down went my roots again, deeper than ever before. I had ten years of bliss before going back to Africa. If you want to know, I went back because I was too happy. I made my own the thoughts of an ancient Irish missionary who wrote:

'For Éire's love I quitted Éire, hard though it was to leave that green-grassed land of Fál and all the friends I left behind me there. I went from Éire of the Kings for love of God, not hate of her. For Christ's sake – though I make no boast of it – have I left the people of the Gael whom I longed to have ever at my

hand. For love of Mary and of Mary's Son have I deserted Éire'.

He had bleeding roots too!

Now that I am old, my mind goes back to the way we used to be, to the saints of the Liberties. For I have known saints, and touched them with my heart and drunk of their spirit. They were children of God, poor in externals but inwardly God's aristocrats. Suffering children, in them was fulfilled Pascal's saying, 'Jesus of Nazareth is in agony till the end of the world. We may not sleep during that time'. Jesus was in agony in these his poor children, members of his body.

They are gone, drowned in the past; but like bubbles in a well they rise before me, their faces, their voices, their hearts. I call them back to life here, for like the world of the Indians in the forests of Brazil, their world is passing away.

CHOSEN OUT

*V*eronica Doyle, mother, had the eager, innocent face of a little girl. Her husband was sick with his nerves; he also had T.B. and an ulcer. Her daughter Molly had suffered a nervous breakdown after she had been attacked by hooligans, and her youngest girl, Frances, was in hospital with meningitis.

'You know, Father,' she said, 'I was only six months married when my husband got T.B. So I went to my Granny Dunne – she was a little woman with white hair and apple cheeks, and who was Dublin down to her toes – and told her the bad news.

'"Veronica", she said, "isn't it well for you."

'Well, I looked at her, thinking that was an awful hard thing to say to a bride. And then she said, "God has big things in store for you, my girl, and he'll give you the grace to bear them all".

'So over I went to Granny Slevin and told her what Granny Dunne had said. And she said, "She's quite right, Veronica. God is after choosing you out".'

Veronica wiped the tears from her eyes. 'Oh, Father, I came from a lovely home. At the beginning of Lent, Granny Dunne used bring down the big crucifix and stand it on the kitchen table. And if any of us said something that wasn't nice, she'd point to the crucifix and say, "Now, now!"

'It was the same during the month of May. She'd bring down the statue of our Lady and the youngest child would crown her with flowers on the first day of May, and we'd say the Rosary before her every night. We do the same in my own home today. Frances brings in pansies from the garden and we let her crown our Lady on the first day of May.'

Veronica went on to tell me of the time she brought Molly to Mercer's Hospital for shock treatment.

'At College Green, she caught hold of the railings and cried, "I won't go. Leave me alone, Mammy. I won't go". I spent half an hour pleading with her. It was no use. Then the Blessed Virgin put it into my head to say, "Molly, God is after choosing you out to bear this cross. God wants you to do it for souls. If you don't, you won't be like St Bernadette or St Thérèse or any of the saints".

'She looked at me for a full five minutes. I had my hands glued to the railings each side of her, for fear she'd run away from me. Then she asked, "Mammy, is that the truth? Is that the truth?" "It's God's truth, pet," I said. And then she came with me as meek as a lamb. Thank God and his blessed Mother, she's a lot better now.'

I thought of St Paul: 'With Christ I hang upon the cross, and yet I am alive; or rather, not I: it is Christ that lives in me'.

The next morning I offered Mass with Veronica, for her and her family. After it she caught my hand and kissed it. My hand! It is I who should have kissed her feet.

THE MOTHER

So many mothers suffer from rascally husbands: shiftless, thriftless and irresponsible. Mary Lambert's man was such, and his children took after him; they were always in trouble. Mary was a living martyr, a saint if ever there was. Her poor hands were crippled with arthritis, but still she washed and cooked and slaved and prayed and loved them all. Once she had been quite pretty. You could see that.

One day I asked her, 'Mary, how do you manage to survive at all?'

She drew in a deep, deep breath and said, 'Ah, Father, when you enlist you've got to soldier. To tell you the truth, if it wasn't for the half-seven Mass and communion every morning, I don't know how I'd get through the day'.

Then – Erin the tear and the smile in thine eye! – she managed a smile. 'Would you believe it, I was once a Royalette. I was. Dancing and kicking my legs on the stage of the old Theatre Royal. And look at me now! Ah, them were the days.'

Why does God allow the Mary Lamberts to suffer so? I might as well ask, Why did he allow his creatures to crucify their Creator? A mystery of love, we say: to save us from ourselves. Maybe he allows mothers to suffer for the same reason: to save their rascal husbands and wandering children. Through the very sufferings inflicted on them they pull their husbands into heaven by the hair of their heads: God uses us to save each other so.

And my Mary Lambert, shall she not dance again? But certainly! Winged and wonderful, in the theatre celestial, let her be prima ballerina in the Ballet of the Angels!

I CAN'T PRAY

She was in bed in the old Coombe Hospital, and the light shone down on her yellow head. She beckoned me over. 'Father, advise me. I can't say a prayer.'

'Not even one?'

'Well, hardly. I try, but my mind just flies about like a crow on a windy day. All I can do is talk to the pictures of the Sacred Heart and the Blessed Virgin in the kitchen. If anyone heard me they'd think I was mad.'

'And what do you say to them?'

'I talk to them the same as if they were there in the room with me. I tell them to look after the baby when I'm going out. And to watch the oven for me. And to help me pay the bills and help Jack to be kept on in Guinness's. Oh, I tell them all my troubles. Sometimes I give out to them, and 'twouldn't surprise me some day if they answered me back. Sometimes, then, I'd sing them a bit of a hymn. But pray? I couldn't pray if you paid me.'

Was she not worth more than very many sparrows?

THE QUART OF WATER

Bill Carbery was old, so old that he had fought in the Boer War and in the Great War. His body was like a chunk of oak but his legs were 'bet', as he put it. As he lived on the top floor of the flats, he could never come down. His daughter, tall and pale as a candle, looked after him.

I used to bring him communion. His flat was spick and span. The range, and everything that could shine, was shining – the old soldier taking care of his kit. He used to tell me stories of his youth, like how they used to catch the landlord's pheasants with peas that were strung on thread and tied to a stake.

One day I said to him, 'Bill, you have no prayer-book. I'll bring you one, and a few other little holy books to help you pass the time'.

Bill grew embarrassed. 'To tell you the truth, Father, I can't read. But I'll tell you what I do do. I drink about a quart of water every night before I go to bed. That wakes me up around two in the morning, and I get out on my knees and say the Rosary, and think a while, and then back into bed. That's the best I can do.'

Old soldier, hard man, survivor of many battles. But the spirit of Patrick and Columcille survived in Bill Carbery.

MY SHAME

At the door of John's Lane church one evening I met an elderly lady coming out. She was shabbily dressed, but a lady nevertheless. I 'put talk on her,' as we say. She told me that in the market that day a youth ran up and snatched her handbag. It held all the money she possessed in the world, twenty pounds.

I, being a carnal man, saw red and thought only of revenge. 'He may escape the police,' I growled, 'but he won't escape the judgement of God.'

She gasped. 'Oh, Father, that's no way to talk! I'm at the loss of my twenty pounds – it's only money. But that poor boy has a mortal sin on his soul. I'm just after lighting a lamp for him now, and praying that God will forgive him.'

I blushed. She was a Christian; I was not. It was as plain as that. The Lord's words lived in her: 'Pray for those who persecute you... Blessed are the merciful, for they shall receive mercy'. To me they were only words...

FROM THE ENDS OF THIS EARTH

The people of the Liberties loved the shrine of Mary, Mother of Good Counsel, in John's Lane. They always ran to her with their troubles. One mother I knew, a soul-friend of Mary, was forced to emigrate to Australia with her family. They were not happy. So this mother dipped her pen in her tears and poured out her soul to the Mother of God – mother to mother.

Dear Mother of Good Counsel,

I, your loving child, Mary E. Sinnott, am writing to you, holy Mother, to ask your loving Son to ask his Father to help me get my family and myself home to Ireland. My children are homesick and so am I, but my husband is terrible homesick. He gets so depressed and often does not talk for days. We are all very unhappy.

Mother, you know I was often hungry in Ireland, but I was never unhappy. We could laugh. I seem to have forgotten how to laugh, holy Mother. You know why I came here: I was worried about my son, Michael. He was only seventeen years and I came to mind his soul that God gave me to mind. I don't know if I did right or wrong. I was worried about Michael's soul, but now I am worried about four souls, as this place is not like Ireland; it is terrible.

Mother, Ireland is heaven. In Ireland you cannot go wrong, as God and the holy Mother are wrapped around you. I never wanted a lovely home; I wanted lovely souls for God. Please, Mother of Good Counsel, help us to get home if it is God's holy will. Please, Mother, I have cried so much. I am crying now. I am all mixed up. Please help me. I have the Novena book; I know your feast day is April 26th and I will pray the prayers every day. Please, Mother, if it is God's holy will.

> *Your loving child,*
> *Mary E. Sinnott, Mother.*

'I never wanted a lovely home, I wanted lovely souls for God...' There is a psalm that says:

O God, hear my cry! Listen to my prayer!
From the ends of the earth I call;
My heart is faint.

St Augustine said, 'When anyone cries from the ends of the earth, it is Christ who cries in him. He is the man with a thousand hearts, a thousand voices'.

With the Mary Sinnotts of the world he is still in agony, and they, with him, are our redeemers.

IS IT ANY HARM?

She was a granny of the Liberties, buxom, blithe and debonair. 'Tell me, Father,' she said, 'is it any harm to be praying always?'

'Any harm? You're a lucky girl to be able to pray at all. Tell me, how do you do it?'

'I can't help it. It's no credit to me. I just can't keep my mind off God, night or day.'

'And what prayers to you say?'

'All kinds. I go to half-seven Mass in John's Lane. Then back home for my breakfast. I sing my hymns while I'm tidying the house – you know, "Hail Queen of Heaven" and "Sweet Heart of Jesus" and so on. You see, I live by myself so there's no one around to mind. Then I set out to do my bit of shopping, and on the way I'm saying the Rosary of the Five Wounds, and the Litany of the Sacred Heart, and the Litany of our Lady, and the Litany of the Tears of Mary, according as they come to me. I know them off by heart with the years.

'On the way back I drop in to the church for half-ten Mass. Then I come home and take up my prayer-books and settle down to my devotions. But my married daughters keep coming in and interrupting me – they can't stay away from me. When they leave it's back to my prayers again.'

'And for the rest of the day?'

'Sure I can't stop, didn't I tell you? I can't keep my

mind off God, in the street or house or anywhere.'

'I suppose you pray in your sleep too?' I said with a smile.

'Troth and I do. I fall asleep saying the Rosary, and I do often wake up saying Hail Marys. I dream regularly about Mary – her standing in a field of corn with the sun shining down on her. Is it any harm?'

'No, girl. It's a blessing from God. Say one for me.'

'Faith and I will, and many a one. I pray specially for priests.'

DOLORES

Dolores means 'sorrows'. She reminds me of Matthew the tax collector. Jesus stopped at the door of Matthew's office, glanced at his ledgers, his receipt books and counters and said, 'Drop all that and come, follow me'.

Like a man in a dream, Matthew left behind his job, his perks, his commission. He left it all. Blind trust! Now he could say, 'I'm a poor man. I have no money. But I am rich for I have Christ'.

Dolores was a mother of five. One child was tragically killed at her door and died in her arms. Then the family had to leave the Liberties to find work in England. From there she used to write to me.

1st April

A long threatening comes at last and here I am, writing again. My poor husband has been very sick since we came over here. He has T.B. and is now in the sanitarium. I have been confined to bed for three months as I am expecting, and all is not well with me. I want you to pray for me.

I am not complaining even though we are very poor. Some time ago my husband was awarded £500 damages in an accident case, but the case was appealed and it is now doubtful if he will get anything.

However, I always say a thousand times, 'Welcome be God's holy will'. I think that the time will never come, God willing, when I can be up and out to Mass and holy communion again, as it's the only life that brings true contentment.

April 20th

How can I thank you for your kind thoughts of me and mine? I have a baby girl three days old, thanks to the almighty, living and true God. The Sacred Heart was very wonderful to me all through my bad time, and I was able to repeat, 'Sacred Heart of Jesus, help me,' all the time. I am in perfect health now, thank God.

I offer up any little sufferings I have in union with Christ's sufferings for the conversion of sinners, for the souls in purgatory and for the Holy Father's intentions. I always offer to our divine Lord all my sufferings for all the times I offend him... I won't forget you in my Masses and prayers, now that I am on the war-path again.

November 2nd

Sorry to tell you that my husband is still in the sanitarium and must have an operation. He was doing very well until he got the 'flu. I tell him not to worry, that God has a plan for us all, and it is really silly to worry. I don't worry seriously about the things of this world any more. I have too much faith in God. The only thing that worries me is to offend God.

Her husband died.

Dolores of the Sorrows! Suffering servant, saving saint, saving souls with Christ! Her pain mingled with the cup of his blood that was shed for all people for the forgiveness of sins.

What a reunion there will be in heaven when all the saints of the Liberties rise up, singing together.

MONICA

She came into the 'box' one Saturday night, a little country woman from out Saggart way, and in the darkness whispered her sad story. She had to go to hospital for an operation on Monday. She was leaving small children behind her, and there wasn't much hope for her. There was an aura of sadness and gentleness about her that went to my heart.

'Look,' I said, 'tomorrow morning I'll offer Mass for you and yours.'

She thanked me, and went on her way. Three months later I received this letter:

Dear Father,

The grace of God be always with you and yours. You may remember to have offered the holy Sacrifice of the Mass for my intentions a few months ago, when I told you I was going to hospital. I was two weeks there, and I am sorry to say they could not do anything for me. But I am sure when God sends anyone of his children any particular suffering, it is for some very special reason of his own, and for our own good and his glory.

When I came back from hospital my little boy, Liam, was in the Children's Hospital. The specialist told us there was no hope of his recovery. Last Wednesday our blessed Lord called him from all his sufferings in this world to his home in heaven. He was just six years old, the eldest of our children. I am sure he is a little saint in heaven, where we trust he will intercede for us all. May God's holy will be done.

Now, amidst all troubles, may God bless and Mary protect you.

After reading her letter I mounted my bicycle and rode out to see her. I met her husband, a small farmer, thin, silent, ascetic. As we talked Monica pointed to a little wooden box under the kitchen table. There was a child's coat in it and a piece of string tied to it.

'That was Liam's little cart,' she said. 'He used pull it around after him. I had taught him that Jesus is everywhere, and he asked me, "Is Jesus in my cart?"

'I said, "Yes, he is". It was a very cold day and Liam said, "Then he must be feeling cold. I'll give him my coat to keep him warm". And there it is.'

There's a gladness in the midst of desolation,
And a glory that shines upon our tears.

Monica has long since followed Liam to heaven. 'I will come again,' Jesus had said, 'and take you with me, so that where I am, you also may be.'

He has no more need of Liam's coat to keep him warm!

THE BLACKBERRY PICKERS

One chilly autumn evening I was walking north along a boreen, out Tallaght way, admiring a yellow moon rise behind a thorny hedge to my right, and a red sun sink behind a thorny hedge to my left. There were no houses then. Out from a gap in the moon-hedge tumbled a little girl, followed by another and another, and then a tiny boy.

'What are you children up to?' I asked.

'Pickin' blackberries, Father,' said the eldest. She was about twelve.

She had a can in her hand, and wore an old hat on her head. The coat she wore, which belonged to her mother, hung down below her knees. Her shins were scratched from the briars, for she wore no stockings, and her feet were wet from standing in the long grass in the ditches, where the raindrops stay all day. In fact, all their shins were scratched, all their feet were wet, and all their noses were cold.

'Did you get many?' I asked.

She showed me the can. It was nearly full, but there were a lot of hard red ones in it, with bits of rusty stems sticking to them.

'Jimmy put in the red ones,' she said. 'There's a bad crop this year.'

'Tell me, how long has it taken you to gather this much?'

'We're out since after school, Father.'
'And how much will you get for them?'
'Two shillings, maybe.'
'And then you can go to the pictures?'
'No, Father. We're putting it in a box to help the priests on the foreign missions.'

They stood around me in a shy little circle. I told them I was a priest from Africa and gave them a little money to buy sweets. They were eager to know about Africa – sunshine every day! – and we talked till the yellow moon was well above the thorny hedge to the right and the red sun was burnt to ashes on the left. As we talked I was thinking of what Francis Thompson wrote somewhere about children: 'Know you not what it is to be a child? It is to have a spirit yet streaming from the waters of baptism; it is to believe in love, to believe in loveliness, to believe in belief.'

Marching homewards, I communed with all the suffering generations who had kept the faith behind such thorny hedges, in little fields like these. These children were heirs to so much: to Christ, to Patrick, to a grace and simplicity rare in this bad world. It is thirty years since I met them, little ships still in the safe harbour of home. Now they are in mid-ocean, and may the Lord be with them.

VISION

I liked to lift people's hearts, because I felt there was always too much of the poor mouth about us: 'Oh, I'll never get to heaven!' Not enough trust and joy in the Lord. So, one Saturday night, when this poor man came in and made his innocent confession, I said, 'You can be a happy man. You have your two feet on the road to heaven'.

'Faith then, Father, I wasn't always a good boy! In my early days I was bad. I done everything.'

'And what changed you?' I asked.

'Well, I'll tell you. I was in bed one night in my room. Was I asleep or awake, I don't know. But I saw the Mother of God standing there with our Lord himself. He turned his back and walked to the door, and he left the prints of his feet on the boards, as if his feet were wet.

'Then his Mother said to me, "Folly them steps. Folly them exactly".

'I tried the best I could, but I was slipping and staggering this way and that. Then she said, "I'll walk them first, and you folly after me".

'She did, and I walked them after her with no trouble at all. Now, Father, was I asleep or awake, I don't know. Was it a dream or a vision or what, God knows. All I know is that that's what changed me.'

Blessed be God! Over the door of the basilica in Lourdes stand the words, *Per Mariam Ad Jesus*: Through Mary To Jesus.

HER PREPARATIONS MADE

Jack Finnegan was a builder's labourer and a bit of a rogue. You had to laugh when you met his blue eyes, dancing with devilment under a shock of red-grey hair.

He and his mates were fond of the odd cup of tea on the job, a practice the foreman frowned on. 'We were buildin' this house,' said Jack. 'The roof was on but it had no ceilin' yet. 'Twas a cold day, so I hung my billycan on a little fire of chips in the fireplace. Well, didn't the foreman spot it. "Now I have you!" he said, and stood with his back to the fire, waiting for the guilty person to own up. Off I went and got a bit of wire and bent a hook on it. Then up the stairs I went with a plank on my shoulders, makin' it look as if I was doin' some work. I let down my hook and drew up my billy and had my cuppa in peace. You should have heard that man when he turned round and found the billy gone!'

Jack lived with his widowed daughter and her children. When he came home in the evening and had his dinner they all knelt for the Rosary. I joined them one evening. It was during the Marian Year of 1954, and Pope Pius XII had composed a special prayer, a very long prayer, full of hard words. Well, I was never so embarrassed: they all knew it by heart except me, the priest!

Whenever Jack switched on a light, his daughter told me, he'd bless himself and say, 'May God give us the light of heaven'. In the mornings after breakfast he'd come out of his room with his cap and coat on. She'd hand him his lunch wrapped in newspaper. Then Jack would place cap and lunch on a chair, and kneel down and say his prayers like a child.

Later Jack got cancer. Poor Jack. The hospital could do nothing for him, so he came home to die. He told me one day, 'You know, Father, a man's mind keeps going back. I'm not a city man. I was born on the mountain above Bohernabreena. After my father died there were only the two of us living in the house, me and my mother. Every Saturday night I used go roving – off to the pub or to a bit of a dance maybe. My mother used get my things ready for Sunday Mass. She'd polish my boots, iron a clean shirt and lay out my good suit. Then she'd wait up for me with a cup of tea.

'Well, this particular Saturday night I knew I'd be back late. So I told her, "Don't wait up for me, Ma. I'll be late".

'Well and good, I went on my way. It was after midnight when I came home. My things were laid out, all neat and tidy, and I noticed the light on in my mother's room. "Ma," I said, "didn't I tell you not to wait up for me?"

'There was no answer. I went into her room and there I found her lying on her back in the bed, her two arms stretched out. Her right arm was through the sleeve of the brown habit – you know the old people were always laid out in the brown habit. Her left hand was holding the

blessed candle, and it had nearly burnt out. And do you know, she had put a basin of water on the chair beside the bed, and held the candle out over it, so that if it fell it wouldn't burn the house down. She was cold and dead. But she had her preparations made. Aye, she had all her preparations made.'

Jack's own hour had come and I was helping him to die. I heard his last confession, gave him his last communion and his last anointing. At the very end, when his feet were cold and the family were praying around him, and I had my hand under his head helping him, he cocked that old roguish eye up at me and whispered, 'Egad, Father, I never thought I'd die with my head in the priest's hand'.

God be with Jack Finnegan. His preparations were made. In Bohernabreena he was born and in Bohernabreena he awaits the resurrection, beside the mother who gave him life twice over.

ON BEING A PRIEST

Because you are a priest the sorrows of humanity come to your door. And the ugliness. And the beauty too, though the beauty may be hidden under ugliness and pain.

A man comes with a broken heart: sorrow has shown him the truth of himself for the first time. And from sorrow beauty blooms: the beauty of repentance, of old wrongs at last forgiven, of humility and faith reviving.

Good people come to be confirmed in their faith that God is with them in spite of all. Weak people, branches almost broken from the Vine, come to be reconciled.

The beauty of being a priest is that so little depends on yourself. You must be a listener, yes, but it is Christ who works through you. It is Christ who reconciles in confession, who comes into the sad heart in communion, who gives the life and love and hope without which we cannot live.

As I write this in 1991, on leave from Africa, I am told that the Irish people have begun the long, slow slide down into apostasy; and that the people of the media, who are hostile to the faith, are doing their best to hasten the decay. Can they not see that a life without Christ is a life without meaning, and leads to chaos and despair?

When I hear a lady on TV, asked if she is a Catholic, reply with immense hauteur, 'No. I am no longer a Catholic. The Church has nothing to offer me,' I feel sad. For she is rejecting, not some abstraction called the Church, but a person: Jesus Christ, Son of God, Saviour.

Against her, accusing her, I place an old African lady who was preparing for baptism. She failed her exam and appealed to me. 'Father! I am old and stupid. I cannot learn like these young ones. My husband is dead. My children are gone from me. I have nothing. BUT I WANT GOD!' She cried it out in her own language: *Niyu ayu Iju!*

It was the cry of a normal person, for the desire for God is natural to the human heart unless it is sick. Jesus said, 'I am the Light of the world'. But, as an inflamed eye turns away from the light of the sun, so a sick heart turns away from the light of Christ.

It is a perilous thing to do, for he also said, 'The judgement is this: though the light has come into the world people have preferred darkness to the light because their deeds were evil'. The one and only cure is the cry of the tax collector in the temple: 'God, have mercy on me, a sinner.'

The people who have spoken in these pages had two things in common: endurance and an iron faith. Faith is a strange gift. It makes Christ present to one: real, alive, breathing, like a person standing at one's shoulder, just out of the line of vision. These people suffered *with* him, which means that they had his breast on which to lay their weary heads, and his heart to murmur, 'I am with you'.

But take away Christ and how do you bear suffering? The unbeliever suffers too, perhaps even more, but he has nowhere to lay his head. Bereft of hope, he may end in despair. And yet to the very end Christ is calling, 'Come to me, all you who labour and are overburdened...'

REUNION

Enough! I have given a few glimpses of the hidden history of the Liberties; talked about a few of its saints. There were thousands more. There are saints still, but they grow old. May the prayers of them all, past and present, save Ireland.

Myself, I am a simple Christian. Naive. Green. A believer. I believe in God's mercy, and I believe in heaven. And I can tell you that one of the things I look forward to is the great reunion with my friends the saints. I shall touch them with my heart and drink of their spirit once more: the old grannies; the Jack Finnegans and Bill Carberys; the Mary Sinnotts, and all the little God-blesha-Father children.

Yes, what a reunion it will be when all the saints of the Liberties rise up, singing together!

BY THE SAME AUTHOR

J34 Lord, Teach Me to Pray
How many times have we wanted to pray but the words just would not come? This little booklet tells us about different ways of conversing with Jesus that leads, ultimately, to a closer union with him.

N47 Restless Hearts
This is the story of one of the most interesting people who ever lived. He was a great sinner, a great genius, a great lover and a great saint. His name, Augustine.

Recommended Reading

J43 That Priceless Treasure – Friendship
by Fr Michael Sweetman, S.J.
Here the author reflects on some of the people whose friendship and influence have greatly enhanced his own life.

Order from: *Postage extra*

IRISH MESSENGER PUBLICATIONS
37, Lower Leeson Street,
Dublin 2.
Tel: 01-767491